Seasoned

poems by

Karen Betz Mastracchio

Finishing Line Press
Georgetown, Kentucky

Seasoned

ACKNOWLEDGMENTS

Grateful acknowledgment is given to the following anthologies in which
these poems have first appeared, sometimes in an earlier version:

Poetry at Round Top 2011—"Wingspan"
Poetry at Round Top 2016—"Rebirth"
A Poetry Society of Texas Book of the Year 2017—"Cleansing"
A Poetry Society of Texas Book of the Year 2018—"Resurrection" and "Smell
of Inspiration"

Publisher: Leah Huete de Maines
Editor: Christen Kincaid
Cover Art: Karen Mastracchio
Author Photo: Elizabeth Ferrio
Cover Design: Elizabeth Maines McCleavy

Order online: www.finishinglinepress.com
also available on amazon.com

Author inquiries and mail orders:
Finishing Line Press
PO Box 1626
Georgetown, Kentucky 40324
USA

Table of Contents

With profound gratitude to family and friends
who have provided the experiences and support
that inspired and framed these poems

Following the Light

Mom taught me about light.
She was not one to keep the house dark,
blinds and windows always opened,
our second home abundant with windows,
filled with light, a large glass door to the patio,
light streamed in from every angle.

Even our tiny first home had a sun porch,
light filtering through screens,
inviting us to play records and dance.
The dusty attic may have housed mice and spiders,
but I recall much more vividly golden dust
illuminated by the sunlight.

So I have been lucky;
from the very beginning I recognized the light.
I knew how to look, where to look.
I understood I had to keep my eyes open,
like the blinds, like the windows,
to let in all the light, then to let it shine.

Memories

Iridescent soap bubbles blown through a wand,
caught in the wind of ongoing life,
drift in the cosmic dust of my mind.
Child me reaches with the wand
trying to take back, hold onto,
the spheres of ephemeral light.
Pop, pop, pop.
Only the residue lingers
on the fingers of recollection.

East/West

Driving at 6:45 a.m. on FM 2920,
blue-gray sky ahead,
pink tinged with gold in my rear-view mirror,
I view fading fringes of night in the west,
dawn's eager advance stretching from the east.

For me, life is that balance.
I focus forward on a road unfolding,
moving toward a goal, a destination,
while the shimmer of life's past always
winks over the shoulder with some brilliance.

The Carolinian

It was crowded with them,
college kids on an early Sunday evening train,
burdened with backpacks and electronics,
returning to some campus, home away from home,
their future, their frustration, their elation.

Their train ride probably averaged two or three hours,
to see parents, to visit high school sweethearts,
pick up cold weather clothes, drop off laundry,
whatever drags them back.

They swarmed on and off
at almost every stop out of Raleigh,
self-assured and polite, willing to help one another,
finishing up papers, checking social media,
plugged in and isolated with a covert eye to those around.

I had forgotten that part of my life so long ago,
the nineteen-year-old riding a packed train,
hustling a cab, three or four of us piling in,
cutting costs, sharing the ride back to our dorms.

We witness what stirs memory,
reminisce about that other time.
I look at them and think how different they are.
I look at them and think how little life has changed.

Tomorrow

Today is all, everything and nothing,
mundane and exceptional,
another sunrise celebrating life.

I greet the day, grocery list in hand,
birds waiting for seed at the feeders,
my small universe open to everything,
perhaps nothing exceptional,
maybe some unexpected mini-miracle,
bumping into an old friend, headache gone, stiff arm limber.

Today my eyes open, my heart opens,
I move one small step at a time from sunrise to sunset.
Tomorrow I will welcome another all-encompassing today.

Gatesville, TX

There is a prison in Gatesville,
a sleepy little town with one main street—
a Walmart, a Beall's, a Subway, a Taco Bell.

Each month Elizabeth and I drove four hours
from Spring to Gatesville, rising early on a Saturday
to be there for the two hour prison visit,

visits with my daughter,
glass or tight meshed wire between us,
sometimes at a table in a small crowded room,

visits as unsatisfying as intercourse interrupted,
feeling the brokenness of relationship,
with no Band-aid in sight to cover the gaping wound.

Still the drives, though long, were lovely—
Highway 107 filled with rolling pastures,
sunlight opening out on green,

gas stops where we grabbed a Frappuccino
in the morning, an Arizona iced tea in the late afternoon,
hitting Cracker Barrel in Huntsville just at sunset.

For three years, one Saturday each month we drove,
four hours there and four hours back,
two hours to visit sandwiched in, imperfect hours.

Those visits forgotten, odd that my memory
holds the beauty of the drive,
the cactus and winding roads near Mother Neff State Park,

fifteen cows lined up outside a mint green farm house,
cool breezes in the small shady park in Gatesville
where we tossed Crystal Stix and loved life.

Stardust

This night sky flawless in its indigo clarity,
stars dapple the velvet backdrop,
stars that form patterns, constellations,
constellations that tell stories
guiding humanity on land and water,
hovering about us, dropping dust
that enters our blood influencing mood and temperament.
At times we credit or blame those stars for our fate.

Cassius knew better,
The fault, dear Brutus, is not in our stars but in ourselves…

Whatever heavenly light has pierced our mortal being
has never bent our free will,
our ability to rise like those stars above adversity.
Like those very constellations,
each of us is given a pattern,
a time and space to blink brilliant, offer subtle radiance,
to take the blessings of our fate,
transcend the obstacles, and shine.

Unfinished Business

Navajo weaving contains a unique thread left loose at the corner of the piece, a blanket or a rug, the "spirit line." Grandmother Spider offered this wisdom—the ability to move from one creation to the next, to keep open one's mind and heart to new work, unborn ideas, and creativity. The unschooled may judge this loose thread, this contrasting line in the weave as a mistake, some unfinished business. Schooled to look for perfection, loose ends tucked in, projects complete, we leave ourselves no room to breathe, no line to find our way forward from success to challenge to success. Checklists of done, done, and done dictate. Stark green lawns polluted with Roundup allow for no dandelions or morning glories, nothing of spontaneous beauty welcomed. Our lives always offering some unfinished business, our spirit line provides our route to each new option, unfinished simply an opportunity.

Smell of Inspiration

A breath, a breeze,
wind rises up from the earth
carrying a scent of loam,
an earthiness that heralds life.
Dirt and water in that smell,
a breeze that with a bit of luck will twist
just so to grab a thread of oleander or jasmine.
My head reels with the floral bouquet
mixed with the heaviness of the dirt and water,
and I breathe, I breathe deeply,
understanding that this breath becomes life in me.
It is inspiration, inspiration to complete old tasks,
to mend a fence, to clean out closets.
It is inspiration, inspiration to start anew,
to write a poem, to love again.
I have breathed in the smell of early spring,
air mixed with earth, water, flowers, and trees,
and I am born again.

Grace

Six white egrets at sunrise land
and stand at the corner of Gosling Road.

What in that vision stirs emotion,
feels like the grace of God poured out?

Even one great white egret
flutters the heart, but six...

a bit like a line of Radio City Rockettes
without the flash, more subtle than all that.

A flood of grace poured out in feathers,
pointed bills pierce the heart in the still morning mist.

Myopic Insight

Age has brought me to a place of altered sight.
Eyes with diminished vision scan light's filtered patterns,
calculating angles of the sun, cycles of the moon.

Hormonal shifts like tectonic plates realign relationships.
Shimmering willow leaves on flimsy boughs
become the beckoning wave of a sometimes friend.

Sight of a kestrel stirs more passion than a lover's kiss.
Daily life splinters into momentary reflections
like shards of shattered mirror under a noon sky,

so that ordinary sights and sounds
ricochet off fragile emotions,
engendering ephemeral depths of joy.

Such myopic vision affords uncanny insights,
knowledge and experience polished by digestion,
a pearl in the oyster rocked in endless, watery sands.

Cleansing

Sleek golden-shimmered grackle,
with a bright eye and a twist of your head,
surveying conditions, you plunge

into the copper-colored basin,
submerging your light frame in shallow tepid water.
Full sun illuminates your toiletry.

Dip, dunk, shake, and fluff.
Feathers plump like porcupine quills
as rhythmic gyrations merge droplets and bird.

In imitation, I shake and shimmy,
a voyeur, more cleansed by your bath than you.

Worst Day

That was the worst train ride...
the worst day of my life...

Sunset Limited was running two hours behind
on a sunny November day,
drawbridge under repair east of New Iberia.
The crew was polite, attentive, apologetic;
the scenery full, meditative—
ponds with yellow flowers skirted by autumn foliage—
not really much to complain about.

> Really? Your worst day?

Remember the day
your first love, one you poured yourself into, moved on,
leaving you in a hole so deep
you couldn't bear to lift the covers.

Remember the day
the brakes screeched outside and you heard the yip,
running you found your dog dead two houses down the street.

Remember the phone call
telling you your child was taken by ambulance
to Ben Taub Hospital, condition unknown.

Remember scrambling to find
money for air fare to Florida
because doctors gave Mom less than a week to live.

> Really? Your worst day?
> ... the train just two hours late

Resurrection

Each day I practice dying.
Sitting cross-legged, I lower my torso,
slowly stretching right leg, then left,
smoothing my spine, turning my palms up.
Lying on frayed carpet in the corpse position,
aches ebb into worn fibers,
tensions leak into carpet padding thinned by life's traffic.
I allow my eyes to open, truer to death than the pose.
As breath levels freeing the muscles, sinews, bones,
Savasana brings vitality.
In this brief death, I find this day's life.

Each day I practice dying.
Blowing out the votives,
I finish my last morning prayer.
Going into my room, I change my clothes,
smooth on makeup, turning my mind to the day ahead.
Leaving home, I bid Elizabeth and the cats goodbye.
I remain myself just awhile, driving in solitude to work.
Pulling into the parking lot, I vanish
as I clip on the I.D. badge that transforms me into Ms._,
forgetting home and focusing on work.
In this personal death, I find this day's professional life.

Each day I practice dying.
At nine each night, I cleanse the day's grime from my face,
brush the meals' residue from my teeth.
I layer lotion, lavender scented, on my drying skin,
inviting sweet sleep with its dreams and healing.
I crunch my pillow and curl on my right side,
waiting with closed eyes to fall back into the womb.
I toss freeing myself from dream to dream,
giving this death no final hold on me.
In stillness of night's waning dark, eyelids flutter open.
Through sleep's death, another day of life finds birth.

The Smell of Hope

After thunder grumbles
and the rain falls hard,
Earth breathes with a freshness,
the smell of hope.

Not the newness of grass
greening in the spring,
nor the full-bodied release
that perfumes autumn's offerings,

it's the cleansing of the sweat and tears
of summer's passion,
innocence baked away
in the sensual embrace of experience,

creating the lust/love counterpoint
that clouds the sky with near regret,
until the clouds break
and shower life's promise.

Rebirth

Bold, bare,
skinny-dipping in a spring-fed pool,
not the taut body of a twenty-year-old,
but mid-life over fifty flesh,
honest, scarred, and worn firm with resolution,
self-consciousness sloughs off like old snake skin.
Nudity of a newborn born again
revels in the cold rush of clear water.

In the Garden

In breathless wonder he stood naked in the garden,
endless green peppered with color,
jasmine reaching high,
wild strawberries under foot,
tomatoes twining upward.

His own small piece of paradise,
he worked steadily season after season,
planting, watering, weeding.
Until through the passage of time,
the garden understood his purpose and love.

Less time each year was required
as birds and squirrels shared in the creation,
not always his vision,
but lush and natural,
fruits and flowers at home among the trees.

On this morning as he watched light beckon life,
he saw it in its fullness.
Feeling the joy and satisfaction
of all the seasons swell in him,
he walked out into the morning naked,
standing breathless in the garden.

Seasoned

In response to Passing a Truck Full of Chickens at Night on Highway Eighty

To see it all and never flinch,

wind in my feathers,
hot, cold, anxious, excited,
I stuck my neck out.

Looking for what?
Five miles down the road
the scenery isn't much different.

Speed brings the rush:
movin', movin', movin'.
If I question,

suddenly all life stops.
Too much introspection
can't be good for a chicken like me.

Flexibility through the bars
has kept me alive
on this ridiculous road trip,

neck craning, eyes ogling,
feathers flying.
When the truck stops,

last looks will season this bird.

Insight

Fleeting images caught by the eye
take refuge in the mind, the soul,
between the time we're born and when we die.

Endless times have I gazed at the sky,
the clouds, the stars, our heavenly goal—
fleeting images caught by my eye.

From earliest breath we strive, we try
to capture each experience despite the toll,
between the time we're born and when we die.

Heart-tug visions will make us cry,
even when we work most to control
responses to fleeting images caught by the eye.

Hello gives way too soon to each goodbye
and life seems broken, seldom whole,
between the time we're born and when we die.

As age encroaches, then, we wonder why
these years have been no light and leisure stroll,
but fleeting images caught by the eye
between the time we're born and when we die.

Surrender

As day wears away
Sun softens, as with age,
less relentless, more relaxed.

Rays of golden light
cast rainbows through windows,
softly embrace plants,

tint the western sky
sometimes purple, sometimes tangerine.
At that sacred time

birds sing farewell to day.
Sun, content to surrender to stars,
to share space with the moon,

moves on to become
daybreak for another nation,
noon in a distant land,

constant light for this solar system,
Earth turning to welcome
endless dawns, endless sunsets.

Whiplash

I was driven by the whip,
keeping boss satisfied, holding on
to the job, to the routine, to the reputation.

Older now, retired, there is no job,
no whip to drive me,
so I sit on the couch suffocating in leisure,

breathing in the nowness of each day,
waiting for the crack of the whip
to startle me from reverie,

to send me scurrying into activity—
get the groceries, mow the lawn, clean the toilets,
visit the dentist, visit the family, do the busyness of life.

Waiting, I sit on the couch in a tee shirt,
no bra, no makeup, no worries,
watching butterflies float in sunlight.

Wrens dust themselves on sandy pavestones,
my eyes drinking in light and shadow,
my hearing compromised,

some sounds clear—wind and birdsong—
others distant and disappearing,
the crack of the whip barely a whisper.

Journey

I left in the flame of autumn,
rolling northeast on the Crescent,
vivid gold, pumpkin orange, flame red
leaves shouting their colors
through Mississippi and Alabama
into Georgia and North Carolina.

I returned through bowers of browned,
deadened leaves, kissed by early frost,
surrendering to natural cycles,
wavering, dropping, drifting until
branch after branch bare themselves,
present bony skeletons—colorless, fleshless, asleep—
holding onto life through thready roots reaching deep.

Letting Go

There's a lethargy to autumn.
Life's last fruit hanging plump,

filled full with spring rain and summer sun,
nearly bursts with the bounty of its purpose.

Still, so long it's held fast to this limb,
cell stem connecting offspring to this tree, these roots.

To drop, to die,
completion of this life cycle—

hesitation hangs bittersweet
as wind cradles and caresses this heavy fruit,

weary fruit willing to feed, yet
reluctant to surrender its sweet life.

Scattered

Flighty thoughts, birds on branches
flutter up, then down, unable to perch.
Restless feathered wings lift lightly
to stir others into random flight.
In November's winds, all is scattered.
Like sycamore branches,
limbs of contemplation rattle and shake.
Leaves of ideas detach, floating into distant yards,
raked and piled by strangers.
I stand bare and thoughtless.

Riding the Peace Train

I want to climb aboard carrying little baggage,
empty hands and open heart,
each of us with no numbered seat,
ready to change places in a blink.

Heading towards joy and peace,
I don't want to round the curve so fast
that the whiplash of disorientation
brings me false ecstasy.

I want to savor the sights,
patiently hear the stories,
followed by the quiet that lets
the click-clack, click-clack become the prayer.

Every one of us, strangers as we board,
will become family before journey's end,
yet part without clinging,
no tears, just peace.

Ticket in my hand, I stand
on the platform,
eyes wide, half smile,
waiting for the whistle.

After Life

A morning late enough for the sun to have stretched
above the horizon, to have dried most of the dew,
to have set warmth in the air, yet
early enough for the birds
to still be singing praise for the sunrise,
to be foraging for breakfast,
to be sounding the alarm of prowling cats,
a morning so beautiful, so ordinary,
that breath quickens, hope leaps,
depression can find no foothold.
A tree, any tree, a single tallow tree stands vigilant,
offering its service to birds, to squirrels, to bees,
not quite fully leaved, in early spring still stretching,
still reaching, smiling at the sun's greeting,
roots wiggling their toes in the moist earth.
I can imagine no heaven more beautiful
than this present moment.
Should my last breath escape now
I would be home.

Homecoming

Long before Dorothy clicked her heels,
chanting, *There's no place like home...*
hearts have beat out that sentiment.

I remember the neon Turtle looming over Ogden Avenue,
making me feel that I had traveled to the ends of the earth,
the Jays potato chip sign lighting the way home,
landmarks long gone.

Deeper in memory is the feel of the air,
crisp and cool on a June morning,
cluttered with lightning bugs at twilight,
the sense of it still present on my skin.

Deeper still are memories of family,
stout ancestors of German and Slovak roots,
peeling potatoes, playing cards, singing carols,
vivid and ever-present.

Wolfe laments,...*you can't go home again,*
memory no match for reality, life ever-changing.
Deep in our hearts we have never left.

Wingspan

Birds' wings, fragile things—
not so, my friend.

Sinews tight, feathered full,
strung strong and light,

cruise brisk air, to hover, to dive,
to cover sweet young in sleep.

When death takes breath,
that weathered wing disintegrates slowly,

reluctant to release
airy visions from layered feathers.

Last Days

End of the week,
       end of the month,
              end of the year,
last days, endings open the door to beginnings.
Good-bye Sunday, hello Monday;
so long April, welcome May.

A bittersweet time, last days
surrender summer's leisure to autumn's schoolhouse,
releasing the hand of the child on her way to adulthood,
last days never the end, simply a transition,
the turn in the poem, an opportunity to see anew
transparent darkness before blinding dawn.

Promise

Naked, emerging from winter's sleep,
each branch forms nodules, buds, bearers of life.
Bud, small embryo, clings to the branch,
branch to the trunk, trunk to the roots.

Curled tight like a closed fist, it holds life in its grasp.
Nourished by rains, encouraged by sun,
each tiny fist begins to uncurl, one finger at a time,
keeping its promise secure.

Hints of green, of red, of gold peek out,
soft and delicate, newborns that they are.
Some catch breath and reach for the sky,
stretching in all directions, waving at the sun.
Others, more reticent, grow slowly, steadily,
clinging close to mother branch.

Each branch, each tree flushes with green, greens with life.
Mid-March welcomes the shimmer, shakes with sneezes.
By April, each individual leaf has taken hands
with brothers and sisters,
forming jubilant dancing circles of shade and shadow,
passing from childhood into adolescence and adulthood.

A wide-open hand, they now fan themselves in summer's sun,
confident in offering the high-five to birds, to squirrels, to me.
I take refuge in the cool of their protection,
so grateful for their gift of life, the patterns they create,
layer upon layer, individual and collective.

When October winds shake and rattle branches,
roots begin to pull color from their countenance;
age fades them, thins them, wrinkles their edges.
I grieve not for their passing, only a transition,
as I stare at baring branches.
Soon the curled fists will offer their hands to me once more.

Born in Chicago, **Karen Betz Mastracchio** was headed for a career in nursing. When she began her college classes at University of Illinois, it was poetry and writing that engaged her and prompted her to change her major. She graduated with a teaching degree in secondary English and a minor in writing. Moving to Texas when she married, she spent the next decade plus raising four children, penning lunch box poems, and lending her volunteer support to many organizations. Once her children were on their educational path, she returned to teaching.

As a teacher, Karen updated her knowledge of the poetry of many contemporary poets as well as revisiting classics. Introduced to new forms and styles, she was excited to share a love of poetry with her students. The endless writing activities and journals reminded her that she enjoyed writing poetry as much as teaching it. New Jersey Writing Project and several workshops at Houston's Inprint expanded her experience and skills. When life slowed down a bit, she was able to focus on the craft, revising and editing many of those student shared writings.

Karen's poetry has been published in various state and national anthologies including *Poetry Society of Texas' Book of the Year, NFSPS' Encore Prize Poems,* and *The Texas Poetry Calendar.* She has been an active member of Academy of American Poets, NFSPS, and Poetry Society of Texas. Karen served for several years as vice-president and program chair for Poets Northwest and is a current member as well as webmistress.

www.ingramcontent.com/pod-product-compliance
Lightning Source LLC
LaVergne TN
LVHW041328080426
835513LV00008B/638